LOOK FOR THE GLIMMERS

101 motivational and inspirational quotes of wisdom

LISA VAN DER WIELEN

LOOK FOR THE GLIMMERS

101 motivational and inspirational quotes of wisdom

There is always a glimmer of hope in every day. May these quotes motivate, inspire and create some glimmers.

LISA VAN DER WIELEN

First Printed 2026

Copyright © Lisa Van Der Wielen

The moral right of the author has been asserted.

All rights reserved.

ISBN: 9781764477017 (Paperback)
ISBN: 9781764477024 (Hardback)

Cover, illustrations and design
by Lisa Van Der Wielen

www.lisavanderwielen.com

People are like books:
Some deceive you with
their cover and others
surprise you with
their content.

Oscar Wilde

Be yourself; everyone else is already taken.

Oscar Wilde

Be the change that you wish to see in the world.

Mahatma Gandhi

Live as if you were to die tomorrow. Learn as if you were to live forever.

Mahatma Gandhi

We accept the love we think we deserve.

Stephen Chbosky, The Perks of Being a Wallflower

Fairy tales are more than true: not because they tell us that dragons exist, but because they tell us that dragons can be beaten.

Neil Gaiman, Coraline

You have brains in your head. You have feet in your shoes. You can steer yourself any direction you choose. You're on your own. And you know what you know. And YOU are the one who'll decide where to go.

Dr. Seuss, Oh, the Places You'll Go!

Life isn't about finding yourself. Life is about creating yourself.

George Bernard Shaw

Success is not final, failure is not fatal: it is the courage to continue that counts.

Winston S. Churchill

Listen to the mustn'ts, child. Listen to the don'ts. Listen to the shouldn'ts, the impossibles, the won'ts. Listen to the never haves, then listen close to me... Anything can happen, child. Anything can be.

Shel Silverstein

You can't live your life for other people. You've got to do what's right for you, even if it hurts some people you love.

Nicholas Sparks, The Notebook

Nothing is impossible, the word itself says 'I'm possible'!

Audrey Hepburn

Do what you feel in your heart to be right — for you'll be criticized anyway.

Eleanor Roosevelt

Instead of worrying about what you cannot control, shift your energy to what you can create.

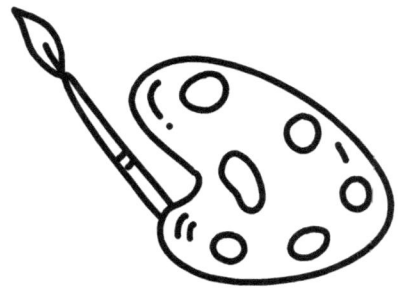

Roy T. Bennett,
The Light in the Heart

Be the reason someone smiles. Be the reason someone feels loved and believes in the goodness in people.

Roy T. Bennett,
The Light in the Heart

Take responsibility of your own happiness, never put it in other people's hands.

Roy T. Bennett,
The Light in the Heart

If you can't fly then run, if you can't run then walk, if you can't walk then crawl, but whatever you do you have to keep moving forward.

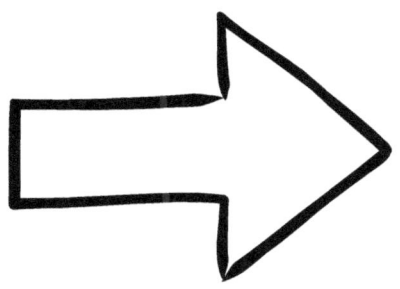

Martin Luther King Jr.

Turn your wounds into wisdom.

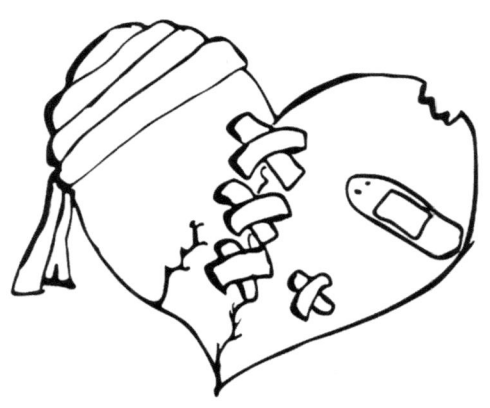

Oprah Winfrey

Keep your face always toward the sunshine – and shadows will fall behind you.

Walt Whitman

No act of kindness, no matter how small, is ever wasted.

Aesop

You miss 100% of the shots you don't take.

Wayne Gretzky

What lies behind us and what lies before us are tiny matters compared to what lies within us.

Ralph Waldo Emerson

The best way out is always through.

Robert Frost

You can never cross the ocean until you have the courage to lose sight of the shore.

Christopher Columbus

Walking with a friend in the dark is better than walking alone in the light.

Helen Keller

Your life does not get better by chance, it gets better by change.

Jim Rohn

Don't let yesterday take up too much of today.

Will Rogers

Don't count the days.
Make the days count.

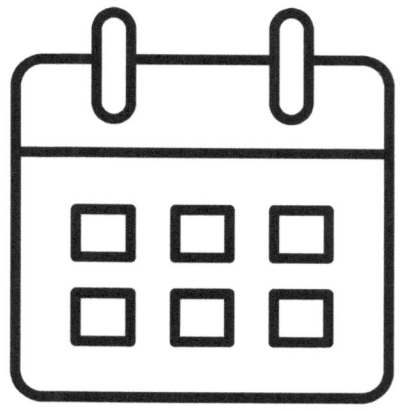

Muhammad Ali

The best and most beautiful things in the world cannot be seen or even touched – they must be felt with the heart.

Helen Keller

Someone is sitting in the shade today because someone planted a tree a long time ago.

Warren Buffett

The best preparation for tomorrow is doing your best today.

H. Jackson Brown Jr.

Shoot for the moon and if you miss you will still be among the stars.

Les Brown

Change your thoughts and you change your world.

Norman Vincent Peale

Let us remember: One book, one pen, one child, and one teacher can change the world.

Malala Yousafzai

Don't be pushed around by the fears in your mind. Be led by the dreams in your heart.

Roy T. Bennett,
The Light in the Heart

Without music, life would be a mistake.

Friedrich Nietzsche
Twilight of the Idols

The future belongs to those who believe in the beauty of their dreams.

Eleanor Roosevelt

Pursue what catches your heart, not what catches your eyes.

Roy T. Bennett
The Light in the Heart

You never fail until you stop trying.

Albert Einstein

Learn to light a candle in the darkest moments of someone's life. Be the light that helps others see; it is what gives life its deepest significance.

Roy T. Bennett
The Light in the Heart

The Chinese use two brush strokes to write the word 'crisis.' One brush stroke stands for danger; the other for opportunity. In a crisis, be aware of the danger--but recognize the opportunity.

John F. Kennedy

Follow your heart, listen to your inner voice, stop caring about what others think.

Roy T. Bennett
The Light in the Heart

If only eyes saw souls instead of bodies, how different our ideals of beauty would be.

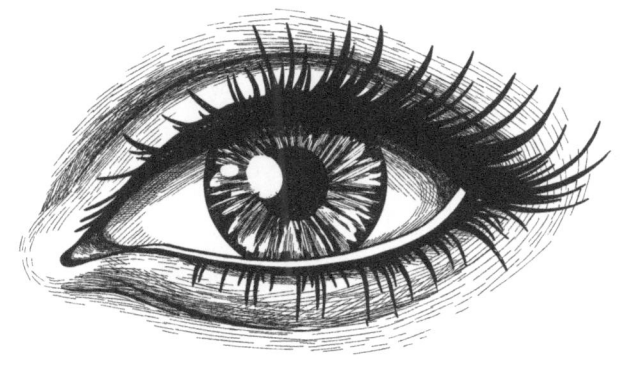

Lauren Jauregui

Water has no effect on fake flowers.

Abhysheq Shukla
Crosspaths Multitude to Success

Those who don't believe in magic will never find it.

Roald Dahl

If someone shows you their true colours, don't try to repaint them.

Dolly Parton

If there ever comes a day when we can't be together, keep me in your heart. I'll stay there forever.

A. A Milne

Give the gift of kindness
in everything you do.
Be the kind of kindness,
you wish to come to you.

Lisa Van Der Wielen

A dog is the only thing on earth that loves you more than you love yourself.

Josh Billings

Sometimes the smallest things take up the most room in your heart.

A. A Milne

The strongest hearts have the most scars.

Jeff Hood

Be who you are and say what you feel, because those who mind don't matter, and those who matter don't mind.

be you

Dr Seuss

We all can dance when we find the music that we love.

Giles Andreae

Life can only be understood backwards; but it must be lived forwards.

Søren Kierkegaard

Life is like riding a bicycle. To keep your balance, you must keep moving.

Albert Einstein

Honesty is the first chapter in the book of wisdom.

Thomas Jeffesron

Success is not the key to happiness. Happiness is the key to success. If you love what you are doing, you will be successful.

Albert Schweitzer

It is our choices that show what we truly are, far more than our abilities.

J.K. Rowling

To live is the rarest thing in the world. Most people exist, that is all.

Oscar Wilde

The purpose of life is a life of purpose.

PURPOSE

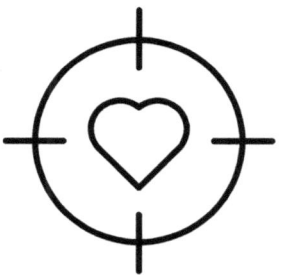

Robert Byrne

That which does not kill us makes us stronger.

Friedrich Nietzsche

The only thing we have to fear is fear itself.

Franklin D. Roosevelt

The best thing to hold onto
in life is each other.

Audrey Hepburn

To love and be loved is to feel the sun from both sides.

David Viscott

Yesterday is history, tomorrow is a mystery, but today is a gift. That's why it's called the present.

Bil Keane

The true sign of intelligence is not knowledge but imagination.

Albert Einstein

Not all of us can do great things. But we can do small things with great love.

Mother Teresa

The only person you are destined to become is the person you decide to be.

Ralph Waldo Emerson

How wonderful it is that nobody need wait a single moment before starting to improve the world.

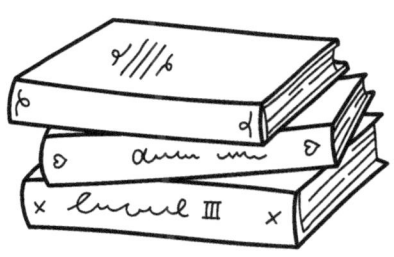

Anne Frank

How wonderful it is that nobody need wait a single moment before starting to improve the world.

Anne Frank

A loving heart is the truest wisdom.

Charles Dickens

Grief is the price we pay for love.

Queen Elizabeth II

Believe you can and you're halfway there.

Theodore Roosevelt

Your worth is not what you have, but who you are.

Matshona Dhliwayo

Stars do not pull each other down to be more visible; they shine brighter.

Matshona Dhliwayo

When all seems to be against you, remember, a ship sometimes has to sail against the current, not with it.

Matshona Dhliwayo

Some people come into your life as blessings. Others come into your life as lessons.

Mother Teresa

Sometimes the wrong things fall apart, so the right things can come together.

Marilyn Monroe

When one door closes, another opens; but we often look so long and so regretfully upon the closed door that we do not see the one which has opened for us.

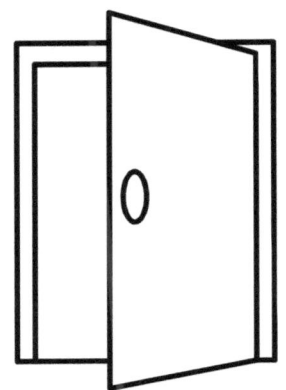

Alexander Graham Bell

Hardships often prepare ordinary people for an extraordinary destiny.

C.S. Lewis

Realize that if a door closed, it's because what was behind it wasn't meant for you.

Mandy Hale

Try to be a rainbow in someone else's cloud.

Maya Angelou

To succeed in life, you need three things: a wishbone, a backbone, and a funny bone.

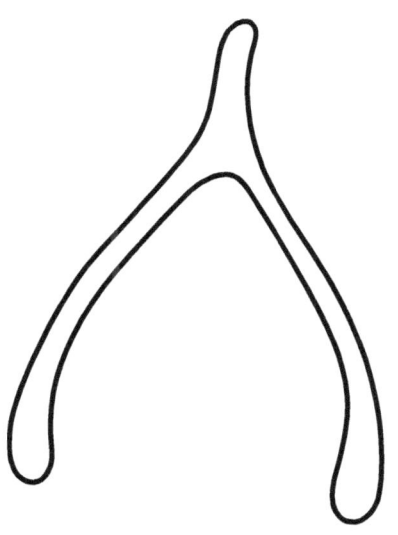

Reba McEntire

The secret to getting ahead
is getting started.

Mark Twain

It is better to be hated for what you are than to be loved for what you are not.

Andre Gide

Get busy living, or get busy dying.

Stephen King

Life is what we make it, always has been, always will be.

Grandma Moses

The secret of happiness, you see, is not found in seeking more, but in developing the capacity to enjoy less.

Socrates

In the long run, the sharpest weapon of all is a kind and gentle spirit.

Anne Frank

If you own this story, you get to write the ending.

Brene Brown

Happy is the man who can make a living by his hobby.

George Bernard Shaw

As you know, life is an echo; we get what we give.

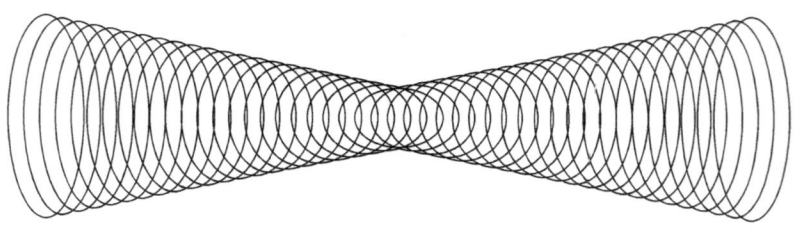

David DeNotaris

Wisdom is not a product of schooling but of the lifelong attempt to acquire it.

Albert Einstein

Worry is a waste of imagination.

Walt Disney

No one can fully understand the meaning of love unless he's owned a dog.

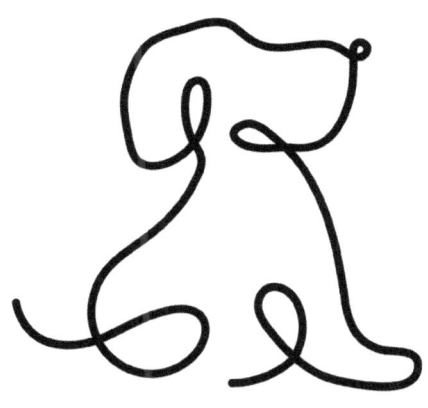

Gene Hill

The highest form of knowledge is empathy, for it requires us to suspend our egos and live in another's world.

Plato

I am no longer accepting the things I cannot change. I am changing the things I cannot accept.

Angela Davis

The real heroism lies in the struggle to be yourself.

Eleanor Roosevelt

Find someone who will sit quietly with you when the world within you is loud.

Unknown

The cave you fear to enter holds the treasure you seek.

J. Campbell

I believe that imagination is stronger than knowledge. That myth is more potent than history. That dreams are more powerful than facts. That hope always triumphs over experience. That laughter is the only cure for grief. And I believe that love is stronger than death.

Robert Fulghum, All I Really Need to Know I Learned in Kindergarten: Uncommon Thoughts On Common Things

Lisa Van Der Wielen is a Primary School Teacher and Author from Perth, Western Australia. Her passions for teaching and writing led her to become a Children's Author in 2017. Her books support the charities Perth Children's Hospital Foundation, Ronald McDonald House and Heart Kids Australia. Her love for the beach, nature, and dogs, provide her with inspiration to write poetry and stories that inspire.
Check out her work on her website:
www.lisavanderwielen.com

There is always a glimmer of hope in every day.

www.ingramcontent.com/pod-product-compliance
Lightning Source LLC
Chambersburg PA
CBHW042117100526
44587CB00025B/4088